T0113561

The Word of God...

A Scriptural Guide for Everyday Living

CHRISTY WIGGINS

ARCHWAY
PUBLISHING

Archway Publishing books may be ordered through booksellers or by contacting:

Archway Publishing
1663 Liberty Drive
Bloomington, IN 47403
www.archwaypublishing.com
844-669-3957

Because of the dynamic nature of the Internet, any web addresses or
links contained in this book may have changed since publication and
may no longer be valid. The views expressed in this work are solely those
of the author and do not necessarily reflect the views of the publisher,
and the publisher hereby disclaims any responsibility for them.

Any people depicted in stock imagery provided by Getty Images are
models, and such images are being used for illustrative purposes only.
Certain stock imagery © Getty Images.

Interior Image Credit: Christy Wiggins

ISBN: 978-1-6657-4282-5 (sc)
ISBN: 978-1-6657-4281-8 (e)

Library of Congress Control Number: 2023907507

Print information available on the last page.

Archway Publishing rev. date: 04/20/2023

CONTENTS

All verses are taken from The Living Bible © 1981

Upper case letters at the beginning of the names for God are a liberty taken by the author.

PREFACE

As we seek to be disciples of Jesus, our humanity haunts us. When we want to be brave in the face of adversity, we find that we are afraid. When we seek to know God, we find ourselves doubting Him. When we interface with the World, instead of bringing forth messages of love and salvation, we often find that we lack the courage and the direction to do so. What is a diligent disciple to do?

We also try to encourage the members of our Christian family as they go about their confusing and often painful lives in this world we must live in today. In fact, the origin of this book is related to this very topic. As I often went about sending comforting cards to people that I knew were in need of spiritual guidance, I began a list of verses that went with certain feelings or problems my friends were experiencing. I then decided to write this book for people to access in times of need. I also hope that the card senders out there will be able to use this way of organizing scripture. Many times, there are no friends near and there's no dial-a-scripture phone service certainly!

I invite you to use this guidebook as an extra person in your life who can be right beside you in your Christian walk. Often, we rely on friends and members of our church families to help us turn our questions into answers of faith that will heal our discipleship or the discipleship of others we love. Most likely and most often, we turn to the Word of God to enlighten us on both occasions.

So, I have written this Scriptural Guide to help readers find their way quickly to the piece of God's Word they may need to hear or share at any given moment. I sincerely hope that the pages and categories included in this guide will help you grow in your Christian life and give you a tool to always shine the light of God's goodness to everyone you know.

"Thy Word is a lamp is unto my feet and a light unto my path." Psalm 119: 105 (TLB)

CHAPTER 1
Knowledge Rules Emotions
(Doubting God)

Mrs. White reluctantly answered the after-lunch phone call. She knew it would be five-year-old Alice's new school. This event was now a common occurrence at the White household.

"Hello! Mrs. White? Alice has bitten another child and this time, yes, she drew blood. You'll have to come get her! Yes, yes, right away please!"

So, in frustration, Mrs. White drives to pick up Alice. The afternoon fun in the park idea flies out of the window of possible plans for a normal day. And as Mrs. White drives, she worries.

"What's to become of her?" she wonders. "Why does she strike out in anger so quickly? Have I been a bad mother? Have I been too strict?"

Read

"Don't worry about anything; instead pray about everything; tell God your needs and don't forget to thank Him for His answers. If you do this, you will experience God's peace, which is far more wonderful than the human mind can understand. His peace will keep your thoughts and your hearts quiet and at rest as you trust in Christ Jesus."
Philippians 4:6-7 (TLB)

Mrs. White's emotions swirl like a whirlwind. They have already begun to destroy her thoughts. 'Don't worry' the scripture admonishes Christians. God knows we are natural championship worriers. We like to fall utterly and helplessly and literally into an abyss of worry. This is where we lose our minds (knowledge) to our hearts (emotions). But in His scriptures, God tells us to use our minds and His teachings to pray and trust Him, and to leave our emotional worries behind. This sometimes very difficult strategy will bring us into the presence of God and His grace. And as we continue to try and solve our problems, God will give us peaceful hearts so that we can approach them with confidence.

CHAPTER 2

Decisions, Decisions, Decisions

(Making Decisions)

Mike knew that he had to choose. He had to get off the fence of safety and jump to either side into the waters of consequences. As far as Mike could guess, either way he went he could be headed for disaster. Should he take the great promotion offered to him from work and move to the big city, or should he stay in Smalltown and keep his three children and their mother happy? The promotion would give him a high standing and well-earned respect within the company. Staying in Smalltown would bring him the same favor with his family. Doesn't family come first, he asked himself as he secretly coveted his dream job in the big city?

Read

"If you want favor from both God and man, and a reputation for good judgement and common sense, then trust the Lord completely; don't ever trust yourself. In everything you do, put God first and He will direct you and crown your efforts with success."
Proverbs 3:5-6 (TLB)

Mike felt burdened by his decision to accept or reject the promotion offered to him at work. But God said, "Trust me!"

Also Read:

"But if anyone keeps looking steadily into God's law for free men, he will not only remember it, but he will do what it says, and God will greatly bless him in everything he does."
James 1:25 (TLB)

CHAPTER 3
Bad to the Bone

(Feeling Guilty)

Sarah could not concentrate at work since the day she had decided to tell lies that cost her coworker, Janet, her job. She was mortified! She could not sleep or even follow the plots that her favorite author wrote. Her guilt weighed on her heavily until sometimes, she even found it difficult to lift her legs and walk.

Why did Janet have to be so mean to her anyway? She started all of this. She started it with her criticisms and snide remarks in front of everyone else. But even weaving justifications, Sarah felt so guilty for her lies that she thought she might just explode.

Read

"Come, let's talk this over! Says the Lord, no matter how deep the stain of your sins, I can take the stain of your sins, I can take it out and make you as clean as the freshly fallen snow."
Isaiah 1:18 (TLB)

Also Read

"But if we confess our sins to Him, He can be depended on to forgive us and cleanse us from every wrong."
1 John 1:9 (TLB)

It is time for Sarah to let go of her guilt and bring it to the Lord. So when Sarah goes into the presence of God, tells Him of her wrong-doing with repentance, God promises He will listen and take her sins away. This has been God's plan since He made the world.

Also Read

"Long ago, even before He made the world, God chose us to be His very own, through what Christ would do for us." Ephesians 1:4 (TLB)

CHAPTER 4
Get Me Outta Here!!!!

(Feeling Depressed)

Thirteen-year-old Melanie was the youngest of four children. Her household was an example of what a beehive might be; people came and went without warning while others played games, made and ate snacks, or watched TV. Melanie often felt lost amid the rather haphazard activities going on in her house. No one seemed to ever sit down and talk to each other or even care how each other's day had been. Especially, she was sure no one cared how she was feeling, or if they even noticed her at all.

One day, Melanie was feeling particularly neglected. She stood in the middle of the living room, took a deep breath, and then shouted, "Will anybody here just slow down for a minute and notice me?"

In all the activity and noise, it seemed no one had even heard her. But her mother heard. She appeared suddenly and wrapped Melanie in a bear hug. "Why don't you go in my room and bury yourself in the covers of my bed like we often do? I'll be there in a few minutes, after you rest, calm down, and pray. Then, I'll join you."

Have you ever found yourself in a tough situation you just knew you'd never get out of, like Melanie?

Read

"I waited patiently for God to help me; then He listened and heard my cry. He lifted me out of the pit of despair and put my feet on a hard, firm path and steadied me as I walked along."
Psalm 40:1-2 (TLB)

I'm sure that Melanie and her mother came to a decision under those protective covers that made Melanie feel more accepted in her own family. Just as Melanie's mother heard her cry during chaos, so it is that God hears our cries.

CHAPTER 5
Give God Just a Little R-E-S-P-E-C-T

(Praise)

Carol and Judy were talking about prayer one day.

"You know, I never can understand that wild praise music that the young people sing now. And then they are quite disrespectful when they pray, don't you think?" asked Carol.

Judy agreed vehemently. "If we don't give out a little old-fashioned respect to God, then to whom?" she asked with disgust. "God is our Father; we should treat Him like a Father!"

Carol nodded her head emphatically. "I promise you are correct! When I pray, I want God to feel honored. Carol paused and then added, "Yet, sometimes, I feel a little empty after praying."

Judy got quiet. She whispered, "I do too. Maybe we can look up some praise verses together and praise God, with humility and respect of course, as we pray!"

Carol's smile grew wide across her face. "Let's do!" she exclaimed as the Holy Spirit beamed from the inside out of her.

I have a feeling that these two ladies have been prompted by the Holy Spirit to join into some much-needed joy.

Read

"Shout with joy before the Lord, O Earth! Obey Him gladly, come before Him with joy.

Try to realize what this means—The Lord is God! He made us—we are His people, the sheep of His pasture.

Go through His open gates with Thanksgiving and His courts with praise. Give thanks to Him and bless His Name. For the Lord is always good. He is loving and kind and His faithfulness goes on to each succeeding generation."

Psalm 100:1-5 (TLB)

(Feeling Pain)

Cindy was in constant pain. Arthritis attacked her joints and made her cane a constant walking companion. Her knees and her hips always cried out for help, and she could not pick up much or bend over very deeply. Her back was a conglomeration of fusions and iron stabilizers. In short, Cindy's daily life became an inconvenience for her painful body.

And so, Cindy came to notice that she seemed to be a lot like the puppet, Oscar the Grouch, and that if they were in contest to see who could be grouchier, she might possibly win. She found that she snapped at people for the smallest things!

Read

"I will say this because these experiences I had were so tremendous God was afraid I might be puffed up by them, so I was given a physical condition which has been a thorn in my flesh, a message from Satan to hurt and bother me, and prick my pride. Three different times I begged God to make me well again. Each time He said, 'No, but I am with you; that is all you need. My power shows up best in weak people.' Now I am glad to boast about how weak I am; I am glad to be a living demonstration

of Christ's power instead of showing any of my own power and abilities."
2 Corinthians 12:7-9 (TLB)

Paul is talking in this scripture about an affliction he had. God would not heal him and so he learned to accept that he had a malady. His steadfast service, even with an ailment, would prove God's power to work in and through His people, even more than if Paul had been perfectly fit.

(Doubting God)

I am Peter, sifted as wheat;
I am John beneath the cross at my Savior's feet;
I am Paul, please pray for me;
For all is dark in Gethsemane.

I try to find You with a prayer;
I blindly reach; You are not there;
I think You have forsaken me;
For all is dark in Gethsemane.

And so I sing my love for You;
For there is naught else I can do;
These words of praise my comfort be;
Here in my dark Gethsemane.

Every one of us has been to the garden of Gethsemane, a place where we are alone and cannot find God. Somehow though, God always finds us.

Read

"Because the Lord is my Shepherd, I have everything I need! He even lets me rest in the meadow grass and leads me beside the quiet streams. He gives me new strength. He

helps me do what honors Him the most. Even when walking through the dark valley of death, I will not be afraid, for You are close beside me, guarding, guiding all the way."
Psalm 23:1-4 (TLB)

CHAPTER 8
Beam Me Up Jesus
(Feeling Impatient)

A group of friends from a retirement community went to lunch one day at the local eatery. They had been discussing the state of the world they live in now.

"I truly don't know what we're going to do!" observed Fred. "I've been here for 75 years, and I've never seen it any worse!"

"I know," agreed Angie. "Little babies dying of gunshot wounds and people are shooting and killing several people at one time without any effort at all!"

"Yes," said Neil. "There's nothing good left. My daughter started housecleaning for the Warrens a month ago and now they've already fired her! Said they couldn't have her telling their secrets all over town! She never even said a word to anyone!"

"Yes, it's true that the world is full of evil," Martin said. "It seems that it gets more and more evil every day. We must keep our eyes on Jesus! And God promises a heavenly reprieve from darkness and sin, and it's okay to look forward to the day when Satan will rule no more."

Read

"And God threw him into the bottomless pit, which He then shut and locked so that he could not fool the nations any more until the thousand years were finished."
Revelation 20:5-6 (TLB)

And meanwhile, we must not forget who we are and what we do.

Read

"You need to keep on patiently doing God's will if you want Him to do all for you that He has promised. His coming will not be delayed much longer. And those whose faith has made them good in God's sight, must live by faith, trusting Him in everything."
Hebrews 10:36-37 (TLB)

CHAPTER 9

But She Would be Perfect for Me...

(Temptation)

Joe is a great guy. He knows it, too. I can do and have anything I wish in this world. I am rich, good-looking, and fun to be around. "And now," Joe said to himself, "I want Alex's wife."

Joe has reasoned it all out. He has noted that Alex casts his wife aside and barely speaks to her. He never gives her compliments or brings her gifts. It's as if Alex doesn't realize what a great wife he has. She's attentive, beautiful, talented, and everyone loves her. What is his problem?

Then Joe thinks about his friend, Alex. They have known each other since grade school. They have had many great times together and Joe really values their friendship.

Read

"But remember this, the wrong desires that come into your life aren't anything new and different. Many others have faced the same problems before you. And no temptation is irresistible. You can trust God to keep temptation from becoming so strong that you can't stand up against it, for He has promised this and will do what He says. He will show you how to escape temptation's power so that you can bear up patiently against it."
1Corinthians 10:13 (TLB)

Also Read

"Be careful—watch out for attacks from Satan, your great enemy. He prowls around like a hungry lion, looking for some victim to tear apart. Stand firm when he attacks. Trust the Lord and remember that other Christians all around the world are going through these suffering too."
1 Peter 5:8-9 (TLB)

CHAPTER 10
Uncle! Uncle!

(Feeling Depressed)

Mr. Roberts got home from work a little early. He settled into his recliner to watch his favorite news show.

"Hi Jacob!" he said as his ten-year-old entered the room. "How was your day at school?"

"It was terrible!" Jacob yelled and then started crying. "I'm being bullied at school, and I need help! But you're always too busy to care!" he finished as he ran from the room.

Even before Mr. Roberts could go after Jacob, his wife came in the room.

"Don't you already know enough about the world without watching this show? And besides, the gutters still need cleaning!"

Mr. Roberts opened his mouth to speak, but it was too late. His wife was gone. He sat down in his chair and put his head in his hands. No matter how hard he tried, these kinds of accusations were an everyday thing lately. Mr. Roberts just felt like giving up.

Poor Mr. Roberts! He was depressed! He couldn't find any answers, and his strength to even look for them anymore was gone.

Read

"He gives power to the tired and worn out, and strength to the weak. But they that wait upon the Lord shall renew

their strength. They shall mount up with wings like eagles, they shall run and not be weary; they shall walk and not faint."
Isaiah 40:29 and 31 (TLB)

Also Read

"Fear not, for I am with you. Do not be dismayed. I am your God. I will strengthen you; I will help you; I will uphold you with My victorious right hand."
Isaiah 41:10 (TLB)

CHAPTER 11

Joe Cool

(The Holy Spirit)

Ted ponders his state as a newly saved Christian. "I just joined the church three weeks ago, but now I'm not so sure. I just have lost my edge, you know. No more cursing or acting cool—no siree! And I miss my old friends and our old hangouts. The Burger Joint down the street used to be so much fun! I could tell all kinds of jokes, whistle at girls, and not care what I thought about. But now, well, now I must be such a goody-goody two shoes!" thought Ted.

Read

"So brothers, you have no obligations whatever to your old sinful nature to do whatever it begs you to do. For if you keep on following it, you are lost and will perish; but if through the power of the Holy Spirit you crush it and its evil deeds, you shall live, for all who are led by the Spirit of God are Sons of God." Romans 8:12-14 (TLB)

Also Read

"If you love Me, obey Me; and I will ask the Father and He will give you another Comforter, and He will never leave you. He is the Holy Spirit, the Spirit who leads into all truth." John 14:15-16 (TLB)

CHAPTER 12

For the Love of God

(Discipleship)

"Well, let's see," mused Amanda. "It seems like an awfully long time since I prayed. When was it really?" she asked herself.

"I don't keep up like I used to," she said. "Why, I can't even remember the last time! Was it this week? Maybe, last? You know, I just don't care as much about it as I used to care. Hmmmm. What did I used to get out of it before?"

Read

"Pray along these lines: 'Our Father in heaven, we honor Your holy name. We ask that Your kingdom will come now. May Your will be done here on earth, just as it is in heaven. Give us our food again today, as usual. And forgive us our sins, just as we have forgiven those who have sinned against us. Don't bring us into temptation, but deliver us from the Evil One. For Yours is the kingdom, and the power, and the glory, forever. Amen"
Matthew 6:9-13 (TLB)

CHAPTER 13
There Must Be More...

(Salvation)

Well, Sunday, I finally gave in. I went up to the front and joined the church. You know I love Jesus. He died instead of me for my sins. That's great! Awesome!

But now that I think about it, I never did hear Jesus say anything. Nothing was really very different when I got into the car and drove home than it had been every other Sunday. I don't look any different. After all, Jesus is the one who is dead. I just believed that He was raised from the dead. But still... I think I should 'feel' different. Did I miss something?

Read

"For God loved the world so much that He gave His only Son so that anyone who believes in Him shall not perish but have eternal life."
John 3:16 (TLB)

This universally well-known verse is true. God says this to us as well.

Also Read

"But if we confess our sins to Him, He can be depended on to forgive us and to cleanse us from every wrong."
1 John 1:9 (TLB)

So, God calls us to confess our sins to Him when and after we have been saved. Although salvation comes to some as a flood of emotional release, to others, it comes as an intellectual choice. But however it comes, continue to abide in God through His Holy Word.

Also Read

"Jesus said to them, 'You are truly my disciples if you live as I tell you to, and you will know the truth, and the truth will set you free.'"
John 8:31-32 (TLB)

CHAPTER 14
I Don't Beat My Wife!

(Virtue)

Jasper was thinking one day about what it means to be good; and especially, if *he* was. He was nearly 70 years old and had just been told that he only had a few short months to live. Jasper had developed cancer in his liver. When we look at his own grasp of goodness, we see that perhaps Jasper had neglected to read the necessary scriptures long ago. Listen.

"Well," he thought, "I go to church, and even tithe. I've been known to give to a charity or two, but I also know that I yell a lot around here at my kids and my wife, and even the dog. But I do pay the bills and put food on the table," he said to himself.

Suddenly, he burst out laughing and when he could catch his breath, he said loudly, "And you know, I don't even beat my wife!"

Read

"And now brothers, as I close this letter let me say this one more thing: Fix your thoughts on what is true and good and right. Think about things that are pure and lovely; and dwell on the fine, good things in others. Think about all you can to praise God for and be glad about."
Philippians 4:8 (TLB)

CHAPTER 15
Hey, Did You Read the Part About...

(Communication)

It got harder and harder for Patti to do her Bible Study every day. Patti was a grade schoolteacher—she liked to sing and talk and interact with others. She was great at it too, but when 10:00 pm rolls around and you're about to do your Bible Study and then go to bed, well, the words 'alone' and 'tired' come to mind.

One night, Patti was reading 1Thessalonians 5:11. And Patti, who did not need much to be talked into gathering a group together, had a great idea!

Read

"So encourage each other to build each other up, just as you are already doing."
1 Thessalonian 5:11 (TLB)

So, Patti texted this verse to a friend. A few minutes later a text came back.

Read

"*Let us not neglect our church meetings, as some people do, but encourage and warn each other, especially now that the day of his coming back again is drawing near.*"
Hebrews 10:25 (TLB)

Patti had to giggle. Now for years, Patti and her friend begin their Bible study together at 10:00 pm sharp. They enjoy the gift of friendship along with the gift of God's word.

CHAPTER 16
Shh! I Hear Him!

(Hearing God's Voice)

Linda prayed at her Community Group whenever they met together. She usually prayed a very traditional prayer; remembering the sick, praying God's blessings on the church, and asking God to uphold their Pastor.

Tonight, she began to pray a little differently. It appeared that the Holy Spirit was helping her pray! The members of the group grew eager with anticipation and put all their attention on God.

"And God," Linda prayed, "we are Your sheep. You are calling us, and we hear Your voice. You have commanded us to give to You what we have in excess. And now You are calling us to do even more. You are calling us to give to the needy and You will bless our gifts exponentially! I have read Your Word, oh God, and now it lives in my heart. Praise be to God."

There was a long silence after the prayer. Then Linda asked everyone to turn to 2 Corinthians 9:12-15. She explained that it was time for the group to begin making plans to bring about a harvest for God. Perhaps it was time to invest time, efforts, and gifts to one of their Church's outreach missions. Maybe the school they supported, or the local homeless shelter would be a good choice. Everyone agreed.

Read

"So two good things happen as a result of your gifts—those in need are helped, and they overflow with thanks to God. Those you help will be glad not only because of your generous gifts to themselves and to others, but they will praise God for this proof that your deeds are as good as your doctrine. And they will pray for you with deep fervor and feeling because of the wonderful grace of God shown through you. Thank God for His Son—His Gift too wonderful for words."
2 Corinthians 9:12-15 (TLB)

CHAPTER 17
Sick as a Dog

(Illness)

Glenda had already lost her job. Her 12- and 14-year-old children tip-toed around her as she lay on the couch in misery, almost wishing she could die. Glenda had Covid; for the second time.

Along with Covid, she had been diagnosed with peripheral neuropathy. This is a difficult disease of the nerves. Glenda remembers joking with her kids saying that they had stepped on her last nerve, but now she knew exactly what that felt like!

So, Glenda had coughed, run fever, and nursed pain throughout her body for eight weeks now. She and her children laughed one after- noon and made up a song:

'I'm sick as a dog;
Can't work or play!
I live in a fog,
Lay on this couch all day.
Whose gonna help me?
Somethin's gotta give!
I'm runnin' out of money,
And this is no way to live!'

Though the song seemed entertaining for a while, soon the feelings of desperation came back to fill the house.

Quietly, young 12-year-old Sarah said one day, "Momma, we're going to pray." And Sarah prayed.

"Dear Heavenly Father, we love and adore You, for You have made us Your own in a world filled with sickness and fear. You have sent Your only Son, Jesus, who healed people wherever He met them while He was here with us. Many of Your children in the Bible wrote about Your faithfulness to heal us even now. In Psalm 46 David said, *"God is our refuge and strength, a tested help in times of trouble. And so we need not fear even if the world blows up and the mountains crumble into the sea." Psalm 46:1-2 (TLB).* And Jeremiah says, *"Nevertheless, the time will come when I will heal Jerusalem's damage and give her prosperity and peace." Jeremiah 33:6 (TLB).*

So, Dear God, whose promises lift our hearts and put our minds on You, we believe and wait for You in our time of trouble. Amen"

A quiet hush fell over the living room as the small, struggling family knelt before God. And peace filled the room. Times were much easier as Glenda healed, got a new job and got on with life. Their life was now filled with strength because once they found Jesus, they never left His side again.

CHAPTER 18
Carolyn Is Confused

(The Holy Spirit)

Julia had known Carolyn for many years. They had gone to the same high school and had been best friends. As time passed by, Julia had joined a church in the community, but Carolyn had not. Though they were still quite fond of each other, they had grown apart because of the different friend sets they enjoyed.

One day long after high school, Julia got a call. It was Carolyn! Julia was surprised and delighted.

"Oh, Carolyn! How have you been doing? I think about you all the time!" said Julia.

"Things are not going so well," said Carolyn sadly.

"Oh no!" exclaimed Julia. "What's wrong?"

"Well, I got fired from my last job. I've had to move out of my apartment and move in with my mother. She's not very happy with me. I knew that you were very tight with God and I called to see if you had any ideas. I'm all out of options and I don't know what else to do!" Carolyn said in a rush.

"Oh no," Julia said quietly. "I do know God pretty well through His Son, Jesus. He helps me when I pray to Him for wisdom and discernment. We could pray together if you'd like," Julia finished.

"Oh, yes, please," Carolyn said excitedly.

(To Be Continued)

Read

"But some will come to me—those the Father has given me—and I will never, never reject them."
John 6:37 (TLB)

CHAPTER 19
Carolyn Meets Jesus

(Salvation)

Later that day, Carolyn came over to Julia's house to pray. They sat together at the dining room table and, at first, considered the situation silently.

"You know," said Julia at last, "you have to meet Jesus before you can talk to Him in prayer. Have you ever met Jesus?"

"Not really," said Carolyn. "Will He even want to meet me now? Will He think I only want to meet Him because I need His help?"

Julia smiled. "Jesus is used to that. Most people come to Him just when they're down on their luck and really need His help. He doesn't mind at all. He never stops loving any of us," she assured Carolyn.

"Okay, well, how do I meet Him?" Carolyn asked.

"Let's start with a Bible verse. The Bible has a lot of Jesus' words inside," Julia suggested. "I know just the verse."

"Okay," said Carolyn eagerly. She had no idea it would be so easy.

Julia opened the Bible and showed Carolyn John 3:16.

"Read this out loud," she instructed.

Read

"For God loved the world so much that He gave His only son so that anyone who believes in Him shall not perish but

have eternal life. God did not send His Son into the world to condemn it, but to save it."
John 3:16-17 (TLB)

Also Read

"God showed us how much He loved us by sending His only Son into this wicked world to bring us eternal life through His death. In this act, we see what real love is: it is not our love for God, but His love for us when He sent His only Son to satisfy God's anger against our sins."
1 John 4:9-10 (TLB)

Carolyn began to cry. "Jesus died for me?" she asked tearfully.

"Yes," said Julia. "He died for all of us. We mourn His death on Good Friday and then celebrate His resurrection on Easter Sunday. It was then that Jesus conquered sin and covered us with His healing blood. Now, God can adopt us into His family because of what Jesus did for us when He died on the cross."

"Oh," said Carolyn quietly. "I didn't realize Jesus actually died for me."

"Yes!" said Julia with a smile. "And He did it because He wanted to!"

Read

"Long ago, even before He made the world, God chose us to be His very own, through what Christ would do for us; He decided then to make us holy in His eyes without a single

fault--we who stand before Him covered in His love. His unchanging plan has always been to adopt us into His own family by sending Jesus Christ to die for us. And He did this because He wanted to!"
Ephesians 1:4-5 (TLB)

Carolyn was crying quietly as she heard these words. She just couldn't believe that God had adopted her as His daughter because of what Jesus had done to save her.

"Now," Julia said quietly, "you ask Jesus to forgive you of your sins. And He will."

And so, Carolyn did.

Read

"If we say we have no sin, we are only fooling ourselves, and refusing to accept the truth. But if we confess our sins to Him, He can be depended on to cleanse us from every wrong."
1 John 1:8-9 (TLB)

"Lord, I have sinned against you, and I have not loved You for all You have done for me," Carolyn prayed sincerely. "Please forgive me Jesus and come live in my heart today. I know now that You died and came back to life for me."

And Carolyn could say no more. The Holy Spirit filled her heart, and she met Jesus.

(To Be Continued)

CHAPTER 20
Carolyn Lives

(Faith)

Carolyn began a new life after she prayed for Jesus to be her friend and guide. The biggest change for her was that she began reading the Bible all the time. She read the New Testament mostly because she was hungry to learn more about Jesus. She wanted to learn about prayer and daily living—all of her new possibilities. And Carolyn started going to church with her friend Julia.

Carolyn loved church. The people who came to church expressed their love for her and their joy at her becoming a Christian. Carolyn grew and prospered under their loving care.

After a few weeks, Julia asked Carolyn to read and reflect on some new scriptures.

"These scriptures will help you to have the wisdom to know what to do about your future," Julia told her. "Of course, God probably won't just appear to you one day and speak out clearly about what you should do about a job. But you will come to know in your mind what it is you should do."

Read

"Dear brothers, is your life full of difficulties and temptations? Then be happy, for when the the way is rough, your patience has a chance to grow. So let it grow and don't try to squirm out of your problems. For when your patience is finally in

full bloom, then you will be ready for anything, strong in character, full and complete."
James 1:2-5 (TLB)

Carolyn that these verses were special to her. She understood that Jesus might not give her a job, but that He would help her figure out the right path as she searched for one. So, Carolyn began to fill out job applications. She wasn't exactly sure which one would be the one that got her the perfect job, but she continued to pray for wisdom.

Also Read

"If you want to know what God wants you to do, ask Him and He will gladly tell you for He is always ready to give a bountiful supply of wisdom to all who ask Him; He will not resent it."
James 1:5-6 (TLB)

Soon, Carolyn got calls for interviews. One for a secretary, one for a receptionist. None of them felt right. Carolyn wanted to serve Jesus now. Those jobs just didn't seem to be the right ones.

One day, she got a different kind of call for a job she automatically thought sounded great! She was asked to interview as a family financial consultant for the Open Homes charity business downtown. She had the background. She knew that she wouldn't make much money, but the job still sounded right to her. When she did the interview, she knew that this was the right job for her. She took the job right away.

Since that day, Carolyn has helped many poverty-stricken families to get on their feet financially. She was able to share her experiences with Jesus and to tell how much He had helped her. It felt good to Carolyn to be living the life she knew that Jesus wanted her to live. And to make a longer story short, Carolyn lived happily ever after.

CHAPTER 21

Not this Girl

(Discipleship)

Shelley was talking to the pastor's wife at a retreat for girls and women at the church. This was not something she would have ever done, but the two of them had adjoining seats at the luncheon.

"Yes, I've enjoyed the retreat so far," Shelley answered shyly. "I've learned a lot!"

Quiet ensued. "What am I doing?" Shelley wondered to herself. "I'll say something stupid I'm sure of it!"

"So Shelley," the preacher's wife began, "What is it that draws you to Jesus Christ, and your new church, WMC?"

Shelley froze for a second. But she knew the answer and began, "Well, it's because here at WMC it seems that people understand how much Jesus loves them."

The preacher's wife smiled broadly. "That's true and we are so glad to have you here."

"And," Shelley began, "We are His…"

Just then, someone came and ushered her partner away. "They need you in the nursery," Shelley heard as they scampered away. She thought that the preacher's wife seemed as disappointed as she was. But in her mind, she finished what she was going to say.

Read

"I am the Good Shepherd and know my own sheep, and they know me, just as my Father knows Me and I know the Father; and I lay down my life for the sheep."
John 10:14-15 (TLB)

And Shelley knew that Jesus was proud. Yes, this girl!

CHAPTER 22

"I'm Strong to the Finich..."

(Despair)

I am waiting: Waiting like many others for surgery. It looms ahead of me but never comes. It is scheduled, but something seems wrong with the calendar. And so I languish in fear and many unsupported beliefs of outcomes I cannot know. I do "eat my spinach," but "That's all I can stands and I can stands no more."

Read

"Don't worry about anything; instead pray about everything: tell God your needs and don't forget to thank Him for His answers. If you do this you will experience God's peace, which is far more wonderful than the human mind can understand. His peace will keep your thoughts and your hearts quiet and at rest as you trust in Christ Jesus."
Philippians 4:6-7 (TLB)

Also Read

"So I pray for you Gentiles that God who gives you hope will keep you happy and full of peace as you believe in Him. I pray that God will help you overflow with hope in Him through the Holy Spirit's power within you."
Romans 15:13 (TLB)

CHAPTER 23
It's so Lame!

(Rebellion)

"You know, James, I really believe that you would like to join the church Youth Group that's near your Grammy this year. Going into the 6th grade is an important time in your life," said Mom.

"No, I don't want to," said James evenly. "That's so lame."

"Oh, I think you would like it," Mom said again. "You would meet new people and the environment would be great for you."

"No, I don't want to," said James. "I wouldn't know anyone there and I don't like the games they play."

"Well maybe you'd grow to like it. You might even get good at the games," said Mom hopefully.

"No, I don't want to," said James.

Later, Mom had errands to run so she left James at Grammy's for a while. James was glad to get away from parental pressure and to watch a little 'Phineas and Ferb' uninterrupted.

Grammy had James' lunch ready, so they talked while he ate. He told Grammy about what was going on at home.

"Oh," Grammy said. "Well, let me see."

After he ate, James and Grammy sat down to watch TV together. While James was occupied with the plot, Grammy had time to make him a simple card. When she gave it to him, he paused the TV and read. When he looked up, he had wet eyes and got up to hug his Grammy.

"You're right Grammy," he said sheepishly. "I love you."

The Card Read

"Honor your father and mother. This is the first of God's Ten Commandments that ends with a promise. And this is the promise: that if you honor your father and mother, yours will be a long life full of blessing."
Ephesians 6:2-3 (TLB)

After the scripture, Grammy had written, "James, I will pray for you every day! I love you! We'll talk next week."

Read

"You children must always obey your father and mother, for that pleases the Lord. Fathers don't scold your children so much that they become discouraged and quit trying."
Colossians 3:20-21 (TLB)

CHAPTER 24

Loser

(Faith)

Andy and Jason were eating lunch at the local bar and grill.

Andy said, "Jason, it looks like you've come to be unhappy since joining the church. That doesn't seem good. Is there anything you want to talk about?"

Jason was ready to talk about this. He had hoped a lot would change when he joined the church, but it had not! "I'm the biggest loser in the world," Jason said. "In fact when I joined the church I had to laugh because losers like me cannot be what God is looking for! I've been laughed at all my life for being a loser; everybody who knows me at all knows it's true. I've been married, now divorced; I used to own my own home, now I rent an apartment, which isn't bad really. My car was repossessed, and I drive a 'hoopty' my brother loans me, and so I just like to come up front and be honest. I'm the biggest loser this side of the Mississippi!"

"You know Jason," said Andy. "I know you well and you are nothing even close to being a loser!"

"Why do you say that?" exclaimed Jason. "It seems I lose at everything I ever try to do!"

"There might be many reasons to claim you can't win," Andy continued, "but you are one of the biggest winners there is! Remember when you were brought into the church you became one of God's children. He claimed you for His own. There is nothing about being a child of God that can make you, or even keep you, a loser."

Jason said, "Well, I kinda know you're right about that. Remind me Andy, how God can take a loser and make him win."

And so Andy got out his Bible and started to find a scripture that he had been wanting to share with his friend.

Read

"Because of His kindness you have been saved through trusting Christ. And even faith is not of yourselves; it too is a gift of God. Salvation is not a reward for the good we have done, so none of us can take any credit for it. It is God himself who has made us what we are and given us new lives through Jesus Christ, and long ages ago, He planned that we should spend these lives in the helping of others."
Ephesians 2:8-10 (TLB)

Jason carefully took the bible from Andy's hands. He read the verses over and over again.

"Well, I don't even have to be responsible for having found the faith to trust God, He gave me my faith!" Jason said with awe. "And then God gave me a new life, not the old one of being a loser. And then He told me something I gotta do. So Andy, I reckon it's time to put away all that silliness of losing and start winning!"

"Well, times-a-wasting!" Andy said. "Let's go on over to the Food Pantry and help unload food boxes to get ready for the next hungry folks that arrive!"

"Well, let's go," agreed a thankful Jason.

CHAPTER 25
Yosemite Sam

(Anger)

Sam and his wife Joanie were playing golf one Sunday afternoon after church. It was a beautiful afternoon with blue skies and the temperature was perfect.

"This is great," Joanie said. "And wasn't church good this morning, especially the three testimonies?"

"Well I'm pretty sure that those three are the present day Pharisees of this world! I hate it when some of those holy rollers get in front of a crowd. They puff up like toads and talk about how good they are," Sam replied with contempt.

"I think they are talking about how God has blessed them. They are talking about what they can do for others using the strength of Jesus," replied Joanie.

"Well, you think wrong!" said Sam with sarcasm. "And how about when they pray? They sound like they know God personally or something. They just make me mad. I tell you, why don't they just let the preacher preach?"

"Wow," said Joanie. "I didn't know it bothered you so much when members of the church gave their testimonies. We are a mission centered church so there are a lot of great stories to share. What would your mission statement be if you could give one?"

Sam didn't have to think very long to answer, "I pray in my closet, I love my God and do what He says, and that's all you need to know about that! Amen!"

"Oh," answered Joanie. "Nice shot," she said as she looked out at the green. "Let's move on to the next hole."

Read

"If you are angry, don't sin by nursing your grudge. Don't let the sun go down with you still angry—get over it quickly for when you are angry, you give a mighty foothold to the devil." Ephesians 4:26-27 (TLB)

I'm glad to say that Sam didn't keep these angry opinions. God spoke, and Sam listened.

CHAPTER 26

Leaving Yosemite

(Reconciliation)

Sam had long resented it when members of the church talked about themselves or prayed in front of the congregation. Sam thought of them as what he called "modern day Pharisees"; always standing in the temple reciting Jewish laws and praying loudly. So without asking for his opinion, his wife, Joanie, had invited over a couple who had done a lot of mission trips for the church. They often shared their experiences with the whole church, which was welcomed and well-received. Well, by most people.

"I surely will be nice," Sam thought to himself. "But I don't have to like them!"

The night arrived and Cathy and Bob came over. Joanie and Sam's house was filled with conversation. Bob told about their mission trip to Ethiopia. He talked about how much the children loved the people who came to minister to them. There were games of tag football and great times of telling Bible stories to them. There were also visits to the hospitals and long hours in the clinic where medical treatment was available.

"Wow, Bob," said Sam respectfully. "You guys really worked hard over there in Ethiopia and brought a lot of joy to the people there. That's quite an amazing thing you did!"

"Oh no, not really," Bob replied. "We were the ones who received the blessing!"

As they were leaving, Sam pulled Bob aside and said, "Bob, I've got to ask your forgiveness," Sam said.

Bob stopped him with a big smile and said, "Sam, I kind of knew you had a problem with me. It's great to know why and become friends. I completely accept your request for forgiveness!"

The two men have become very good friends since that evening. But probably the most amazing part of this story is that Sam lost his anger. No one really knows where it all went, but everyone was thankful, especially Sam himself.

Read

"Dear brothers, don't ever forget that it is best to listen much, speak little, and not become angry; for anger does not make us good, as God demands that we must be."
James 1:19-20 (TLB)

Also Read

"Try to stay out of all quarrels and seek to live a clean and holy life, for one who is not holy will not see the Lord. Look after each other so that not one of you will fail to find God's best blessing. Watch out that no bitterness takes root among you, for as it springs up it carries deep trouble, hurting many in their spiritual lives."
Hebrews 12:14-15 (TLB)

CHAPTER 27
Worry Wart

(Worry)

Mom called that morning.

"Hello?" Krissy answered.

"Just calling to see how my Worry Wart is," said Mom.

"Oh Mom, you know I don't worry! I *care*," said Krissy.

"Okay," answered Mom. "So, tell me what you're 'caring' about these days."

"Well," began Krissy, obviously launching into a long list, "there are quite a few things. In fact, I'm caring so much these days that I can't even care for myself!"

"Oh dear!" Mom said. That sounds little like worry."

"Oh no, Mom. It's not. But just let me tell you. I find out tomorrow if I have Alzheimer's. You know they can test that now with a spinal tap. Well, my spinal tap was six weeks ago, so naturally, I've been thinking about it every day since then. And there's this girl I know at work. She told everybody to pray for her, but she wouldn't say why. So now I've been caring about what could be the problem. And then, yesterday, I went to the dentist with a toothache, and he said I would have to have a root canal. Oh, good grief, that sounds scary. I haven't even gotten an appointment yet, so I'll be having to think about that until they finally call with one for me. Then I'll need to prepare myself for the procedure itself. Well, Mom, I guess you can see that I'm overwhelmed!"

"I see", said Mom with a sad smile.

Read

"Open the gates to everyone for all may enter in who love the Lord. He will keep in perfect peace all those who trust in Him; whose thoughts turn often to the Lord. Trust in the Lord always for in the Lord Jehovah is your everlasting strength."
Isaiah 26:2-3 (TLB)

CHAPTER 28

Momma Told Me Not to Come!

(Discipleship)

The Johnson family had just moved to a new neighborhood, so Keith was new to his church, but everyone seemed really nice. He had already been invited to a Christian Boys Gathering which made him very happy. They were scheduled to meet once every other week at a participant's house. The gathering was at George's house this time. George was a guy that Keith had come to like very much.

When he asked his mom if he could go, she said, **"Keep your eyes open for spiritual danger; stand true to the Lord; act like men; be strong; and whatever you do, do it with kindness and love." (1Corinthians 16:13-14 TLB)**

"What does that mean?" exclaimed Keith.

"That all just means don't do anything there that you wouldn't do if Jesus was there too. That's all," his mom replied.

"Oh," said a relieved Keith.

So Keith's mom dropped him off at the Gathering the following day. Keith felt nervous as he entered, but everything seemed fine. George's mom welcomed him and brought him into the den where everyone was snacking and talking. Keith joined in without hesitation. George's mom left the room.

Here was some of the conversation that Keith heard:

"I know I don't like our preacher either; he's a dork!"

"Yeah, I think the Youth Pastor has a really cute daughter! I'd like to get a date with her just to see how far I could get..."

"I really hate Sunday School. Let's see if we can find a secret place to hide and maybe our teacher won't miss us!"

"Are you going to the school dance? I hear that somebody is bringing cigarettes."

Keith went to the bathroom and called his mother. "Come get me," he whispered into the phone. "I promise you; Jesus is not here!"

Read

"You have been Christians a long time now, and you ought to be teaching others, but instead, you have dropped back to the place where you need someone to teach you all over again the very first principles of God's Word."
Hebrews 5:12-13 (TLB)

Also Read

But you are not like that, for you have been chosen by God Himself—you are priests of the King, you are holy and pure; you are God's very own—all this so that you may show to others how God called you out of the darkness into His wonderful light."
1Peter 2:9 (TLB)

(To Be Continued)

CHAPTER 29

Mother Bear

(Discipleship)

Mary was new in town. Her family was trying a new church. They had attended several times and the pastor and his wife seemed very strong in the Christian faith. In fact, everyone in the church seemed very loving and spiritual, and the best part was that during the sermon, Mary felt the Holy Spirit stir with joy inside her.

So Mary was very surprised when her son had come home from a boy's Gathering, telling her of rampant disrespect for the church and even God, Himself.

Mary was now attending a Couples Gathering to see what exactly might be going on. The men had gotten into their own groups to talk about man things, but there were many groups of ladies that Mary could join. She passed by one group that was gossiping about church members, one that was planning this week's dinners, and another was talking about how there were no Bible Study Groups on Sunday nights any more.

Mary was not a timid soul. She grabbed a glass and tapped on it with a knife until all was quiet. "*So no one can become my disciple unless he first sits down and counts his blessings—and then renounces them all for me* it says in *Luke 14:33 (TLB),*" she announced to the group. "Ladies and gentlemen," she continued, "We must be more like Jesus than like the general public, you see. Jesus says, "*No one can be my disciple* who does not carry his own cross and follow me." *Luke 14:27 (TLB).*

There was a silence over the crowd for several minutes. Then Mary offered, "I will have you all over to my house for the next Gathering if you like. So, on Wednesday after next, I'll see you there! Right now, I must go. It was great getting to know you all!" And Mary left.

Read

"Quietly trust yourself to Christ your Lord and if anybody asks why you believe as you do, be ready to tell him, and do it in a gentle and respectful way."
1 Peter 3:13 (TLB)

(To Be Continued)

(Discipleship)

Mary and her family had been going to a new neighborhood church since a recent move. The church seemed to be filled with loving people and the pastor seemed like a strong spiritual leader. But as Mary had come to know the congregation, she realized that there were many problems that lurked beneath the scenes.

"However," Mary had said to herself, "there are so many good people here is this church."

She was having a group meeting for couples, called a Couples Gathering. This meeting, she had announced, would be different from the typical Gatherings everyone was accustomed to. In fact, Mary was unsure if the meeting would be well-attended. But she was ready.

Soon her living room was full of people. Extra chairs had to be brought in. So as people took their seats, they found Bibles scattered all around.

"Welcome all," smiled Mary. "I have a countertop full of snacks that we can enjoy after we meet with Jesus."

The gatherers looked around the room and some of them scoffed. There didn't seem to be any 'Jesus' in the room. Mary noticed all of this and said, "Oh, He'll be here later."

Mary's meeting was a success and Jesus *did* come by *and* He brought God and the Holy Spirit with Him. The time was right. The congregation had all missed God. All God's children were longing for time spent in His presence.

They all read and discussed at length some very important verses in the Bible.

Read

"When I think of the wisdom and scope of His plan, I fall down on my knees and pray to the Father of all the great family of God—some on earth—that out of His glorious unlimited resources He will give you the mighty inner strengthening of His Holy Spirit. And I pray that Christ will be more and more in your hearts, living within you as you trust Him. May your roots go down deep into the soil of God's wonderful love and may you be able to feel and understand as all God's children should how long, how wide, how deep, and how high His love really is, and to experience this love for yourselves though it is so great that you will never see the end of it or fully know or understand it. And so at last you will be filled with God Himself."
Ephesians 3:14-19 (TLB)

There were many transformations in Mary's living room that evening. Praise be to God!

CHAPTER 31
The Little Engine

(God is Able)

Wanda had thought of herself since childhood as the little engine that could. Raised on the same story, of the little engine working hard to get her toys to the little children on the other side of the mountain, Wanda believed that a person could do just about anything if they tried. And Wanda tried many things.

During her career, Wanda had been a teacher, a sales clerk, a dog trainer, and a hair dresser. She had lived in and renovated eight houses which in the end, she flipped for a profit. And the hobbies Wanda had started over the years were breath taking. She quilted, knitted, dabbled in stainded glass, and tye-dye and she had taken time to cook a few recipes very well. But, Wanda just couldn't find anything that interested her very much for very long.

"I wonder why I can't settle down?" asked Wanda to herself one day as whe was buying paints for her new hobby, paint-by-number. "Oh well," she would muse, "I've really enjoyed a myriad of places and projects during my life!"

There were a few things Wanda stuck to like glue. Her marriage—she'd been married for thirty eight years—and her church. She had attended and served as a Sunday School teacher in the same church for thirty of those thirty eight years. All of Wanda's friends admired her for sticking tightly to these very important lifelong commitments. Wanda knew that *she* had not accomplished such loyalty and devotion. Wanda knew, as she had always known, that God is able.

Read

"*And now all glory to Him who alone is God, who saves us through Jesus Christ our Lord; yes, splendor and majesty, all power and authority are His from the beginning; His they are, and His they evermore shall be. And He is able to keep you from slipping and falling away, and to bring your sinless and perfect into His glorious presence with mighty sounds of everlasting joy. Amen.*"
Jude 1:24-25 (TLB)

CHAPTER 32
What's Next?

(Discipleship)

Joyce had been a Christian for long time. She had attended church and raised her children there. She had volunteered some; did Vacation Bible School a litte, and had been on some prayer retreats with youth groups. Now that her children were gone, Joyce wonered what was next in her life. How could she serve the church now?

Joyce began to pray. She widented her horizons to include her community and her city. Serving the Lord seemed possible outside the church as well as inside. In fact, Joyce decided serving in the community gave her a chance to be like the disciples. Jesus appeared to them after the crucifixion and told them this:

Read

"You are to go into all the world and preach the Good News to everyone, everywhere."
Mark 16:15 (TLB)

So Joyce decided to investigate her church's list of mission outreach activities. She found one she liked very much. The church had adopeted a school where students generally struggled to read on grade level. This seemed like a rewarding activity! Joyce joined the school as a volunteer right away.

Two years later, Joyce still volunteers at the school and reads with children twice a week. She remembers the story of the disciples who were rowing their boat during a storm. They feared they would capsize, but Jesus appeared walking on the water toward them. At first they were afraid, but Jesus calmed them with His voice.

Read

"Then they were willing to let Him in, and immediately the boat was where they were going."
John 6:21 (TLB)

CHAPTER 33
Critical Christine

(Sin)

Christine had always enjoyed being around people. She liked to join groups so she could get to know other people. She was active in her church and attended as many activities as she could.

Christine and her husband Matthew had recently joined a gaming night in their neighborhood. They were getting to know their neighbors better. Even though they had lived next door, or on the same street for months or even years, they did not know very much about each other. Every night after gaming, Christine would come home full of opinions, talking about the neighbors she'd encountered there.

And Matthew would listen.

"I just can't stand the way Linda thought she was right about every subject that was brought up tonight! She claimed to know all the rules to Dominoes but nobody was sure how to play the whole night. How did your table do Matthew?" Christine said one night after they had come home.

"We did fine," Matthew mumbled. He had enjoyed his evening.

"Well, our table stayed confused," Christine said. "And then, Linda started the conversation at breaktime about the lawn care people and how they should cut the bushes the right way this spring. Maybe we shouled just let her cut them herself, huh?"

Matthew was silent as he listened. "Christine loves to get out and go to all of these social events," he thought to himself, "but she doesn't seem to really enjoy being around people at all."

So Matthew said aloud, "Christine, why to you go if you have to criticize everyone so much?"

"I don't know," Christine replied with a shrug. "Maybe I don't like people as much as I thought!"

Read

"Anyone who says he is walking in the light of Christ but dislikes his fellow man is still in darkness. But whoever loves his fellow man is walking in the light and can see his own way without tumbling around in darkness and sin."
1 John 2:9-10 (TLB)

CHAPTER 34
All Is Lost

(Faith)

Fifteen-year-old Jamie was very discouraged. She had been contemplating for weeks now how it seemed hopeless to find any genuine goodness in the world anymore.

"Mom, I don't think good can win at all in this world. Evil is so strong and is so much in control! I am beginning to think that the whole world is evil," she began on afternoon.

"Well," her mom replied. "That's a severe assessment, Jamie. Where do you see all this evil?"

"I see it in abused children's cases and in the wars across our world. I see it when families are killed in automobile accidents and even at school when kids are mean to other kids for no reason," replied Jamie. "I even see it when I ask for help in class and the teacher ignores my needs because she is talking with some of her 'favorite' students."

"Yes, Jamie, I see it too," answered Mom. "It is the nature of this world we live in to harbor evil people and bad events. But I've seen a lot of times that good has been the victor over evil. Abused children often find safety and love in a new family or a group home. People heal after losing loved ones in car wrecks and live happy lives. And you will be shaped and molded by your encounters with evil. You will grow to seek out love as God taught us it should be and practice the love of God with everyone you know. Jamie, did you know that because you have seen the darkness, you can now become a light? And soon, as you shine, you will see that others shine with you, and the darkness does NOT win. So, take heart, my sweet girl," her mother finished.

Read

"Before anything else existed there was Christ with God. He has always been alive and is Himself God. He created everything there is—nothing exists that He didn't make. Eternal life is in Him, and His life gives light to all mankind. His life is the light that shines through the darkness--and the darkness can never extinguish it."
John 1:1-5 (TLB)

CHAPTER 35

Dexter Decides

(Why Bad Things Happen)

Dexter had been an atheist almost his whole life. He made a conscious decision about his stance on religion early in his life. You see Dexter was a twin. When Dexter and his twin brother were about eight years old, a drunk driver ran into their car on the driver's side. Both Danny and his mother were killed in the accident. Only Dexter survived.

Dexter's Dad did the best he could after the whole horrible incident was over. He was devastated by the loss of his wife and son. Now it was just him and his only son Dexter.

Many years passed. Dexter's Dad never remarried and tried hard to work and be a good role model for his son. These things were challenging. He often wanted to give up. But he kept on trying until his only remaining son graduated from high school and went his own way.

Dexter loved his father and was glad to have had his love all the years of his life. But he blamed God for taking his family from him.

"No father would allow such a thing to happen to his family," Dexter reasoned. "Therefore, there must be no God."

But Dexter could no longer hear the Holy Spirit, who leads us in all truth.

Read

"He is the Holy Spirit, the world at large cannot receive Him, for it isn't looking for Him and doesn't recognize Him. John 14:17 (TLB)

However, Dexter always thought that there was more to life than just being born and dying. He had learned early on about God from his mother before she died. She had taught him to sing 'Jesus Loves Me' and to thank God for all their blessings in life. But all of that had been put aside in the wake of his mother's and brother's deaths. For many years, he could find no blessings to thank God for at all. But, yet he wondered and considered what might really be the truth.

Dexter was hearing God's call to him even though he didn't know it. Dexter may have forgotten God, but God did *not* forget Dexter. Dexter decided to open a long neglected piece of his mother's inheritance—her Bible. The Bible was well used and obviously had been studied thoroughly. There were notes in all the margins in his mother's handwriting. Dexter was captivated by one particular note. It said, "God finds his children no matter where they wander". The verse was in the book of John. So Dexter read it several times because he felt a little lost himself.

Read

"My sheep recognize My voice and I know them, and they follow Me. I give them eternal life and they shall never

perish. No one shall snatch them away from Me. For My Father has given them to Me and He is more powerful than anything else, so no one can kidnap them from Me. I and the Father are one."
John 10:27 (TLB)

(To Be Continued)

CHAPTER 36
Dexter Rethinks

(A Lost Sheep Found)

When Dexter read these words from his mother's Bible, Dexter felt a lot of things all at once. He felt the presence of his mother and his twin brother. And he felt the presence of God. He had been lost for so long. But still, there remained a grudge.

"If Jesus loves me so much," he wondered aloud, "why did He take away the most important people in my life just when I needed them most? I don't know any other men who have had to go through what Jesus has sat back and watched me endure!"

Dexter once again flipped some pages. He found a verse marked, 'Beware!' He decided that this had to be important, so he read…

Read

"*Last of all I want to remind you that your strength must come from the Lord's mighty power within you. Put on all of God's armor so that you will be able to stand safe against all strategies and tricks of Satan. For we are not fighting against people made of flesh and blood, but against persons without bodies—the evil rulers of the unseen world, those mighty satanic beings and great evil princes of darkness who*

rule this world; and against large numbers of wicked spirits in the spirit world."
Ephesians 6:10-12 (TLB)

Dexter felt a lot like crying, but he hadn't cried since the double funeral so many long years ago. He now realized now that in this world of unexpected and sometimes difficult circumstances that God was still in control. He knew that God had not taken his mother and brother from him, nor had the drunk driver. It was the natural rule of evil in the world that had taken them. Dexter realized that the world we live in is ruled by Satan. He felt relieved because he knew that his mother and his twin were with Jesus now. One day, he realized, if he could find his faith again he could be there with them one day. Dexter flipped back a page. In the margin were his mother's words, "why we do it".

Also Read

"And I am sure that God who began the good work within you will keep right on helping you grow in His grace until His task within you is finally finished on that day when Jesus Christ returns."
Philippians 1:6 (TLB)

So, Dexter prayed for Jesus to begin again and to finish in him what He had started when Dexter was a small child. And in that same moment, Jesus rejoiced because one of His lost sheep had finally come home.

CHAPTER 37
Worried William

(Fear)

William worried. It was who he was. Anyone who knew him knew that at any given time, Will was worried. Will worried about everything from his finances to his health. He just couldn't stop.

But one day, Will realized all his worry was pointless, he realized that faith and trust overcame worry. He found this faith while reading an old story in the Bible he had forgotten about. He read about Jairus in Chapter 5 of the Gospel of Mark.

You see, Jairus' daughter was dying. Jairus knew that only Jesus could save her, so he set out to go to the lake where Jesus was teaching. When he saw Jesus, he implored Him to come with him to save his daughter who was at the point of death.

And Jesus started to go with him. But the crowds were large and their needs many. A woman touched His cloak and was healed. Jesus stopped to talk with her. Just then, a messenger brought news that Jairus' daughter was already dead. It would be too late for Jesus to come. But Jesus looked at Jairus and said, "Don't be afraid. Just trust me."

"Ahh!" William thought as he read this. "Will it work? Should he just trust Jesus?" And he quickly went on the read the rest.

So, when they arrived at Jairus' house everyone was crying and grieving. They didn't believe that the little girl was only sleeping, as Jesus told them. Jesus took the parents and three disciples up to the little twelve-year-old girl's room and said to her, "Get up little girl."

And she did.

Will put down the Bible with a great sigh. He though about Jairus waiting on Jesus to go with him to his house and how every second counted to get there before she died. Yet Jesus seemed unconcerned, and even stopped to heal someone else and then to have a conversation with her.

"Jairus must have been beside himself with worry," Will thought. "Wow! I'm going to start telling myself what Jesus said to Jairus: 'Don't be afraid. Just trust me' and throw all my worry out the window." And so, Will did just that.

Read

"For the scriptures tell us that for His sake we must be ready to face death at every moment of the day—we are like sheep awaiting slaughter; but despite all this overwhelming victory is ours through Christ who loved us enough to die for us. For I am convinced that nothing can ever separate us from the His love.
Romans 8:36-37 (TLB)

CHAPTER 38
One More Christmas

(Grief and Loss)

Margie had been taking care of her husband Frank for many years. In the beginning, she had been with him through all the many doctor's visits and together they had hoped for better times. Then, Frand began to forget things. Soon he forgot who he was. Somehow, he always knew Margie. He always knew that she would take care of him.

And she did. In the end, Margie kept Frank at home until his last days. It was summer, and she knew then that he would not see the next Christmas as she had hoped. But she cherished all her remaining time. Margie's daughter came to stay with her and help with responsibilities for her dad.

A neighbor came to see how things were.

"Hospice gives him only 24 to 48 hours," Margie told her neighbor tearfully. And they prayed.

"I see him in the garden," the neighbor prophesied. "They are walking together, he and Jesus, hand in hand in the garden." And they cried together.

The next evening, though it had not rained, the neighbor saw a beautiful rainbow over the neighborhood and knew that Frank had gone to be with Jesus in the garden.

Read

"And now, dear brothers, I want you to know what happens to a Christian when he dies so when it happens, you will not be full of sorrow, as those are who have no hope. For since we believe that Jesus died and then came back to life again, we can also believe that when Jesus returns, God will bring back with Him all the Christians who have died."
1 Thessalonians 4:13-14 (TLB)

And Jesus spoke to the repentant thief on the cross and said, "Today you will be with Me in Paradise. This is a solemn promise."
Luke 23:43 (TLB)

CHAPTER 39
Insider Advantage

(Prayer)

Susan often prayed for people. And she always knew that in some way, her prayers were answered. She knew that maybe they would not be answered as she had prayed them, not in her way, but in the Heavenly Father's way. She knew this because she had an insider advantage. She had the Holy Spirit praying with her.

Read

"And in the same way—by our faith—the Holy Spirit helps us with our daily problems and in our praying. For we don't even know what we should pray for, nor how to pray as we should; but the Holy Spirit prays for us with such feeling that it cannot be expressed in words. And the Father, who knows all hearts knows, of course, what the Holy Spirit is saying as He pleads for us in harmony with God's own will."
Romans 2:26-27 (TLB)

So Sue asked to join her church's Prayer Warriors group because she wanted to help others through her prayer. The prayer list came via email every Monday.

As Sue read over the list, certain people's names and their needs really spoke to her heart. She chose those names to pray for that week. It seemed clear to Sue that these people belonged in her prayers. She began each time by praying the prayer that Jesus taught His disciples to pray.

Read

"Our Father in heaven, we honor your holy name. We ask that your kingdom will come now. May your will be done on earth, just as it is in heaven. Give us our food again today, as usual, and forgive us our sins, just as we have forgiven those who have sinned against us. Don't bring us into temptation but deliver us from the Evil One. Amen."
Matthew 6:9-13 (TLB)

Then Sue carefully and thoughtfully added the names she had chosen. And she knew that in His way, God would bless the people on her list.

CHAPTER 40

People Talking Cannot Hear

(Seeking Direction)

All her life, Jan had done the right thing. She had obeyed her parent and done well in school. When she heard the voice of Jesus calling her to repent and come to God, she obeyed. Ove the years, Jan had studied the Word of God, gone to church, and live a solid Christian life.

After Jan retired and was rattling around the house all day, she thought God was calling her to serve Him.

"So, what do I do?" she thought to herself.

Jan started talking about what sorts of things she could do. She talked to everyone she knew about their opinions of what volunteering venue would fit her the best.

"I could tutor, or I could volunteer at Food Banks. Maybe I could go into Nursing Homes to offer aid and comfort." She speculated one day, "I could even be a missionary!"

Jan continued to pray and read God's word. She put her faith in God and stopped talking about her future long enough to listen to God.

Read

"I will bless the Lord who counsels me and gives mew wisdom in the night. He will tell me what to do."
Psalm 16:7 (TLB)

Also Read

"And now may the God of peace who brought again from the dead our Lord Jesus Christ, equip you with all you need for doing His will. Pray He who became the first Shepherd of the sheep by an everlasting agreement between God and you, signed with His blood, produce in you through the power of Christ all that is pleasing to Him. To Him be the glory forever and ever. Amen"

Hebrews 13:20-21 (TLB)

CHAPTER 41
Carolyn the Cowardly Lion

(Trusting in God)

Janet was alone in the house. She was sitting quietly after a busy afternoon of cleaning. Suddenly, she decided to pray. She felt that God was listening to her. She began to feel His presence in the very house she was praying in, even in the very room.

Janet grew afraid. She quickly rose and closed all the blinds and doors as if to keep God out. Surely God was too good to come into her house to see her as she really was!

Then she remembered reading in the Bible about when Jesus came to the shore where Simon Peter was cleaning his nets. His livelihood was in desperate trouble, and he was worried. Then Jesus appeared on the shore and asked if He could borrow the luckless fisherman's boat to speak from, for a crowd had gathered on the beach to hear Jesus teach. Thinking his boat should be at least good for something that hopeless day, Simon Peter said that he would row Jesus out a little ways to teach.

After teaching, Jesus told Simon Peter ton cast out his nets one more time to gather fish. So, reluctantly, he did. But this time and in no time, Simon Peter's nets became so heavy and full of fish that they were in danger of tearing. When he called for help, James and John, his fishing partners and friends came rushing to pull their boat up beside his. But soon their boat was also full of fish. Both boats were so full of fish that they seemed in danger of sinking!

Read

"When Simon Peter realized what had happened, he fell on his knees before Jesus and said, "Oh sir, please leave us—I'm too much of a sinner for you to have around."
Luke 5:8 (TLB)

    Then, Janet knew the reason for her fear. "Oh, God! I am afraid of You because You are so good, and I am just a sinner!"

    And just as Jesus had calmed Simon Peter's fears, He calmed Janet's. Janet heard Jesus in her heart as He said the very same words to her that He had said to Simon Peter.

    "Don't be afraid."

Also Read

"We need have no fear of someone who loves us perfectly; His perfect love for us eliminates all dread of what He might do to us, and shows that we are not fully convinced that He really loves us. So you see, our love for Him comes as a result of Him loving us first.
1 John 4:18-19 (TLB)

CHAPTER 42
William Works
(Encouragement)

William was forty-seven. He was a very typical husband and father of three. He went to work every day so that his family could prosper. And even though Will enjoyed providing for his family, he grew weary of working.

"I can't believe how much I work!" Will would say. "I never stop!"

Will's wife, Sally, was a stay-at-home mother. She took care of the home and the kids diligently. She was active in the school that her children attended. Sally also got everybody up and dressed to attend church on Sunday mornings.

One particular Sunday morning, Will griped, "I work hard all week and then on Sunday, my rest is taken from me! Doesn't God promise to take care of us? What about the sparrows of the field? They don't seem to work very hard. They just hang out and sing all day!"

Read

"Don't be afraid of those who can kill only your bodies—but can't touch your souls! Fear only God who can destroy both soul and body in hell. Not one sparrow (What do they cost? Two for a penny?) can fall to the ground without your Father knowing it. And the very hairs on your head are

numbered. So don't worry! You are more valuable to Him than many sparrows." (TLB)

"Yes," Sally reminded him. "God does talk about taking care of the sparrow. But when He begins the story, He talks about what can destroy not only your body. What God seems to really be talking about here is how much He cares for our souls."

"Maybe…" began Will.

"And there's more," Sally said. "You have to read 1 Timothy.

Also Read

"But anyone who won't care for his own relatives when they need help, especially those living in his own family, has no right to say he is a Christian. Such a person is worse than a heathen."
1Timothy 5:8 (TLB)

"And so, you see," said Sally fondly, "you work so hard to take care of us here at home. And we are proud of you for that," she said grinning.

And Will was so encouraged that he didn't complain about work any more for a long time.

Also Read

"So encourage each other to build each other up, just as you are already doing."
1 Thessalonians 5:11 (TLB)

CHAPTER 43
Carolyn Is Confused

(The Holy Spirit)

Julia had known Carolyn for many years. They had gone to the same high school and had been best friends. As time passed by, Julia had joined a church in the community, but Carolyn had not. Though they were still quite fond of each other, they had grown apart because of the different friend sets they enjoyed.

One day long after high school, Julia got a call. It was Carolyn! Julia was surprised and delighted.

"Oh, Carolyn! How have you been doing? I think about you all the time!" said Julia.

"Things are not going so well," said Carolyn sadly.

"Oh no!" exclaimed Julia. "What's wrong?"

"Well, I got fired from my last job. I've had to move out of my apartment and move in with my mother. She's not very happy with me. I knew that you were very tight with God and I called to see if you had any ideas. I'm all out of options and I don't know what else to do!" Carolyn said in a rush.

"Oh no," Julia said quietly. "I do know God pretty well through His Son, Jesus. He helps me when I pray to Him for wisdom and discernment. We could pray together if you'd like," Julia finished.

"Oh, yes, please," Carolyn said excitedly.

Read

"And in the same way—by our faith—the Holy Spirit helps us with our daily problems and in our praying. For we don't even know what we should pray for, nor how to pray as we should, but the Holy Spirit prays for us with such feeling that it cannot be expressed in words."
Romans 8:26-26 (TLB)

CHAPTER 44
Carolyn Meets Jesus

(Salvation)

Later that day, Carolyn went over to Julia's house to pray. They sat together at the dining room table and considered the situation silently.

"You know," said Julia at last, "you have to meet Jesus before you can talk to him in prayer. Have you ever met Jesus?"

"Not really," said Carolyn. "Will He even want to meet me now? Will He think I want to get to know him just because I need His help?"

Julia smiled. "Jesus is used to that. Most people come to Him when they need His help. He doesn't mind at all. He never stops loving any of us," she assured Carolyn.

"Okay. Well, how do I meet Him?"

"Let's start with a Bible verse. I know just the verse," Julia suggested.

"Okay," said Carolyn. And Carolyn read where Julia pointed.

Read

"For God loved the world so much that He gave His only Son so that anyone who believed in Him shall not perish but have eternal life. God did not send His son into the world to condemn it, but to save it."
John 3:16-17 (TLB)

Also Read

"God showed us how much He loved us by sending His only Son into this wicked world to bring to us eternal life through His death. In this act, we see what real love is: it is not our love for God, but His love for us when He sent His only Son to satisfy God's anger against our sins."
1John 4:9-10 (TLB)

Carolyn began to cry. "Jesus died for me?" she asked tearfully.

"Yes," Julia replied. "He died for us all. We mourn His death by crucifixion on Good Friday and we celebrate His resurrection on Easter Sunday. It was then that Jesus conquered sin and covered us with His healing blood. Now, God can adopt us into His family because of what Jesus did for us on the cross.

"Oh," said Carolyn quietly. I didn't realize Jesus actually died for me."

"Yes," said Julia with a smile. He did this because He wanted to."

Read

"Long ago, even before He made the world, God chose us to be His very own, through what Christ would do for us; He decided then to make us holy in His eyes without a single fault—we who stand before Him covered with His love. His unchanging plan has always been to adopt us into His own family by sending Jesus Christ to die for us. And He did this because He wanted to!"
Ephesians 1:4-5 (TLB)

Carolyn was crying quietly as she heard these words. She just couldn't believe that God had adopted her as His daughter because of what Jesus had done to save her.

"Now, said Julia tenderly, "you ask Jesus to forgive your sins. And He will."

And so, Carolyn did.

Also Read

"If we say that we have no sin, we are only fooling ourselves, and refusing to accept the truth. But if we confess our sin to Him, He can be depended on to forgive us and cleanse us from every wrong."
1 John 1:8-9 (TLB)

"Lord, I have sinned against You and I have not loved You for all you have done for me," Carolyn prayed sincerely. "Please forgive me Jesus, and come live in my heart today. I know now that You died and came back to life for me."

And Carolyn could say no more. The Holy Spirit filled her heart, and she met Jesus.

CHAPTER 45

Carolyn Lives

(Faith)

Carolyn began a new life after she prayed for Jesus to be her friend and guide. The biggest change for her was that she began reading the Bible all the time. She read the New Testament for she was hungry to learn more about Jesus. She wanted to learn about prayer and daily living and all of her new possibilities. And Carolyn began going to church with Julia.

Carolyn loved church. The people who came to church loved her and would tell her that they were glad she was a new part of their family. Carolyn knew this by reading the Bible, but she really experienced it by being in church.

After a few weeks, Julia asked Carolyn to read and reflect on a few new scriptures.

"These scriptures will help you have the wisdom to know what to do about your future," Julia told her. "Of course, God probably won't just appear to say what you should do about a job. But you will come to know in your mind what it is that you should do."

Read

"Dear brothers, is your life full of difficulties and temptations? Then be happy, for when the way is rough, your patience has a chance to grow and don't try to squirm out of your problems. For when your patience is in full bloom, then you

will be ready for anything, strong in character, full and complete. If you want to know what God wants you to do, ask Him, and He will gladly tell you, for He is always ready to give a bountiful supply of wisdom to all who ask Him; He will not resent it."
James 1:2-5 (TLB)

Carolyn believed that these scriptures were special to her. She understood that Jesus might not give her a job, but would help her figure out her correct path as she searched for one. She continued to pray for wisdom.

Soon Carolyn got calls for interviews. One was for a secretary job, another for a receptionist. None of the interviews felt like she should take the jobs if they were offered. They just didn't seem quite right.

One day, she got a different kind of call for an interview. She automatically thought it sounded good. She was to interview as a financial consultant for The Open Home charity business downtown. She had the background. She knew she wouldn't make much money, but it just sounded right. When she went to the interview, they offered her the job right away. Carolyn said yes.

Since that day, Carolyn has helped many poverty-stricken families to get on their feet financially. She has been able to share her personal experiences with Jesus and to tell how much He had helped her. It felt good to Carolyn to be living the life that Jesus wanted her to live.

CHAPTER 46

The Sparrow

(Witnessing)

A sparrow on the windowsill?
I glance up in surprise;
It is so cold and he so small;
How will the bird survive?
He flies away to worlds unknown
To seek a crumb of bread.
With courage born of desperate hope
The little sparrow flies.

But when the winter is bitter cold
And windowsills are few
And no one reaches out their hand
The little sparrow dies.

And there are tears in Heaven
To see the sparrow fall,
Because his guardian angel knows that the sparrow's least of all,
For the angel sees our brothers who have never heard God's call,
Yet he weeps and prays the winter will not make the sparrow fall.

For God guards each flight taken
By the sparrow in His land.
What care that He has taken
To mold each by His own hands!

But we are far more precious
Than a flock of sparrows are
And God desires to give us Bread
So we may never die.

So share God's love with others
Holding out the Bread of Life;
Without us they won't hear the news
Of life through Jesus Christ.

And scatter bread in winter
On your lawn for sparrows small,
So you won't forget your brothers who have never heard God's call,
For they are hungry like the sparrow but don't know the way at all,
Will we weep and pray the winter will not make our brothers fall?

Printed in the United States
by Baker & Taylor Publisher Services